Afterglow

*I Pam
Gyda'm cariad a'm diolch,
Aled xx.*

Aled Lewis Evans

ℂℙ

Cestrian Press

First Published in 2021 by:
Cestrian Press
13, Stanton Road,
Bebington,
Wirral.
CH63 3HN

©Copyright 2021
Aled Lewis Evans

The right of Chester Poets to be identified as authors of this work has been asserted by them in accordance with the Copyright, Designs and Patents Act 1988.

All Rights Reserved

No reproduction, copy or transmission of this publication may be made without written permission. No paragraph of this publication may be reproduced, copied or transmitted save with the written permission or in accordance with the provisions of the Copyright Act 1956 (as amended).

First Published 2021

978-0-904448-61-0

Printed and bound in Great Britain by Book Printing UK,

AFTERGLOW

Many thanks to Morelle Smith, Kemal Houghton and Caroline Wilson for their assistance and encouragement during the preparation of this poetry collection spanning the last decade.

Thank you to Chester Poets for publishing some of these poems over the years in their various Anthologies. I'd like to thank the constant encouragement of this wonderful group of poets and performers, people who have always responded so warmly to my work.

Aled.

CONTENTS

Foreword   xi

Comments by Welsh Poets   xii

Places in Wales   -   -   -   -   13
Skateboarding   -   -   -   -   14
Virtual   -   -   -   -   -   15
Summits   -   -   -   -   -   16
Spring   -   -   -   -   -   26
Waldo Williams   -   -   -   -   28
Andrea Bocelli   -   -   -   -   29
Venice Sunny Afternoon   -   -   -   30
Ramblas   -   -   -   -   -   31
Church of St Hywyn, Aberdaron   -   -   32
Cymraeg Welsh   -   -   -   -   33
Cymru   -   -   -   -   -   36
Eurwen   -   -   -   -   -   37
Good Samaritan   -   -   -   -   39
Palm Sunday   -   -   -   -   -   40
With These Hands   -   -   -   -   41
Only the Nailing   -   -   -   -   42
Resurrection   -   -   -   -   -   43
Llandaf Christ -   -   -   -   -   44
Pennant Melangell at Easter   -   -   45
Superhero   -   -   -   -   -   46
Welsh Learners   -   -   -   -   47

Pennard in June	48
The Peacemakers	50
These	51
Welsh Poets on the Street	52
Same Time Each Year	54
Surrender	55
School Reunion	56
Pontio	57
Breathe	58
Aunty Gwyneth	60
Erddig	62
Grass Cutting in Bangor is y coed	64
Butterfly for Bet	65
Pilgrimage	67
Pools	69
Salem	70
Dolwreiddiog	72
Fluent	73
Connections	75
Four More Sleeps	76
Damaged	78
Mother Teresa	80
A Church in Monaco	81
Playing for Me	82
Inis Faithleann	84
Signs	85
A Necklace of Stars	86
St Martin's in the Field	88

The Garden Behind the Theatres	89
Tide Turning	91
Stereophonics in Wrexham	92
Indian Summer	94
Last Day of the Holiday	95
Aberfan 1986	96
Despite the Sun	97
Editing	100
Minority	101
Equality	103
Scouse	105
Second Chance	106
Could Have Beens	107
Starlings	108
Long Road Ann Griffiths	109
The Photo	110
Unknown in Ardudwy	112
Visiting Yr Ysgwrn	113
Waiting	114
Welfare House	116
Willard White Concert	117
High Bridges	118
There is Still That Feeling	121
No Man's Heath	123
Tell Me on a Sunday...please	124
Advent in Chester	125
Christmas Concert at the Parish Church	127
Eagles Meadow Fountain	128

Light	129
Mair Coedpoeth	130
The Minister	132
Finale	134
Reunion	135
The One	137
Waiting in the Wings	138
Where Was Jeremy Kyle When You Needed Him?	139
Mary and Joseph in Spar	141
Keeping the Idea Alive	142
Darren	143
Requiem for Emma	144
Valle Crucis Abbey	146
Flow of Divine Dee	147
The Angel	149
Index to Titles of Poems	150

FOREWORD

Aled's poetry sees through the veneer of our fractured, blemished and alienated lives to what is heart-filled, eternal and uplifting. He has a gift for seeing the spiritual in the everyday world, particularly in nature – the new buds, the blossoms, low winter sunshine, the illuminated sea.

His poems often come across hidden and unexpected jewels, behind exterior displays. In human beings he reveals, beyond our all-too-human facades, the vulnerabilities and hopes of the human heart. In the outer world there are sanctuaries, sacred wells, and 'alcoves and arbours' in The Garden behind the Theatres. Aled's poems have the capacity to "see into the life of things" as Wordsworth said in 'Tintern Abbey'.

Like the butterfly in Butterfly for Bet, he explores paths and passages
>'between the shroud of the curtain
>and the spontaneity of the breeze'

With great insight and sympathy, he writes of those who have left us, often prematurely, and those who are left behind; he sees the potential, the fire and the light.

Morelle Smith.

Poet, Travel Writer and Editor

COMMENTS BY WELSH POETS

'In those 'unexpected' moments – from New York to Wrexham – Aled Lewis Evans finds the strength of his faith and his hope in a church, at a funeral or on a trip abroad... this is a candid and gentle collection which nevertheless looks under the skin of the modern world. And despite the dark shadows, marvels at the 'necklace of stars'.

Iwan Llwyd (gwales.com)

Skateboarding:
'The poems are all snapshots of the experiences – but these are no conventional snapshots. Instead, we see the artistry of a photographer whose camera looks beyond what is usual, giving a different slant, finding meaning and image in both the most ordinary and extraordinary of things. Every picture clear and lucid, and printed on the film of vers libre.'

Ceri Wyn Jones

'Vers libre is his medium; and he uses it extremely deftly and effectively ...'

Einir Jones (Barddas)

PLACES IN WALES

There are still places in Wales
not noted on today's maps,
Tom Tom technology
found them too difficult to discover.

Perhaps that's how
these areas are able to survive,
a mystery to modern media.

Little roads that no one knows of their existence,
triangles to disappear into between
Llangernyw, Trofarth
Betws yn Rhos.

Rhyduchaf, Maes y Waun
Llidiardau.

At Cefn Canol we are warned
"Drive carefully"
there is no chance of any other way.

Places that virtually nobody
goes through,
only people like me.

Triangles between Cwmpenanner,
Llanfihangel Glyn Myfyr
and Cefn Brith.

At Sycharth, Llansilin, Rhydycroesau,
vast acres of our will to survive,
here on an ancient border.

Our best kept secrets.

SKATEBOARDING

Dreams boarding a skateboard,
yearnings set free there,
to collect money,
go somewhere far enough away
from here.

Life is motion.

Problems boarding a skateboard,
Image, being young,
maintaining 'street cred' with the Park gang;
placing obstacles there
that can be skateboarded by,
not like life.

Memories and frustrations
get a small space on board the skateboard.
Remembering the part-time work in London
delivering parcels on the bike,
before it was stolen.

And now you're back
in the hunger of a storm about to break
in rural Wales.
How much longer can you skateboard
to your future?

VIRTUAL

Your life is always elsewhere,
on your phone,
real or imaginary
(I'm not quite sure which).
In all your holiday-mode haste,
a great deal is ignored,
always smiling at your WhatsApp feed.

You seek Wi-Fis of approval
in cafe corners,
not engaging in real conversation
face to face.
On screen you offer intimacies that are not
intimate at all
and don't fulfil you.
But that's how it is.

I am invisible
here before you,
offering more
than all the screen flicks can offer,
if only you'd raise your gaze.

SUMMITS
In memory of Ben

PLATEAU

He wasn't an angel,
but he was an angel to someone.
In childhood photos
he looked like an angel to everyone.

He loved going on the 'bike' at Tywyn,
scooting along, gripping tight.

Then slowing to follow a hearse
past the empty caravans.
Following death one January.
He liked his Nain's house.
Then overtaking on the A55.

Overtaking death for now.

SEEING

Cyrn y Brain a back-drop for the uniform estate
Ben wanting to take the Holy Grail to the top of his Dinas Brân.

Escape to the slag heaps.
"That bike'll be the death of him one day" -
the throw-away remark.

The bike which travelled the tumps of Pandy,
teasing the gravelled graves of Gresford.

On the bike he'd come alive,
a giant
ruling the world,
adventure lighting up
the dullness of his eyes.
Then, on the innocent motocross
of the silent tips
he'd think things possible,
That preserving 'cred' of the Caia Kids.

A different view from the top of the tips.

GRAFFITI

The bite of the first ground frosts
the hoar clinging on,
and the stubborn warmth of the bright sun along the roads.

The berries are red this year.
The red of your young loss,
The red-eyed bewildered mother,
The red horror of an accident.

Little Ben
framed on the mantelpiece.
Your sunset a youthful red
unforeseen,
penetrates like these November rays.

In your absence you draw me
to that old merry-go-round
of bitter, difficult feelings
trying to understand life lost
on the cusp of your eighteenth year.

On the walls of the shop over the road
the graffiti of Ben's peers,
abbreviated notes of grief.
"See U Wen we get there" and a Cross.

An early November sunset
giving the edge to red.

ROLLERCOASTER

Some live your sort of life,
life at speed.
Like a rose pruned before it blooms
expiring before it buds,
and its giddy rollercoaster
reaching the depths
and then screaming to the heights,
the momentary delay
before thundering to the waiting pit.
There are some who live like you,
Ben from the Caia.

A mother spins on the whirligig of grief,
at times drowning in her remaining family,
in the daughter who came home from Rhyl.
But other times crossing the road
and still seeing the graffiti,
gagging on the Caia Kids' tribute.

The times when a full house is not enough
the tea drinking
the fag smoking.
For those days

when it never stops raining,
for those gaps
in the conversation.

At the times before the rain eases
before the sun reluctantly
drags itself from behind the clouds.

On the Cefn Road,
a drooping sunflower.

HELMET

Children in Need Day,
A concert and commotion over in Town.

"I can do everything, but I can't go and get his clothes back from the hospital."
Buried in a tracksuit,
with trainers, and the new watch he got
for his seventeenth.

The policeman arrived with his helmet this afternoon
the family fingered it tenderly
recalling Ben with a smile and story

The Caia Kids want to see him again
in his coffin at Pentrefelin.
"He's not an exhibit"
His mam loses patience with the over-familiar
vicar with his incessant jokes.
"You're not going to piss around in the funeral, are you?"
He sees there's no point in crossing her.
"Cracking jokes and all that".

A mother in need tonight.

THE FUNERAL

Amidst the bare branches
a hearse of realisation glides inexorably,
local press cameras keep their distance
but their prying lenses whisper secrets,
and the curtain falls.

Reaching the church, apprehensive
of delivering this most difficult of orations
for Ben and his Mam and to the Kids of Caia –
a service for a church full of Ben's contemporaries.

The Vicar, so dignified today,
and the softer side of the estate
maligned by all,
flooding every corner.
Four hundred Caia Kids
filling St Giles'
  unsolicited.
A sea of trainers and unsinging baseball caps
from the highways and byways
with their hymn-less youth and their quiet tears.
Today, heads bowed,
searching for a grain of meaning
from somebody somewhere.

Then they came to the cemetery,
to see that release
into the lonely dark hole
today so deep
to the generation of evergreen magazines.
No one deserves to die at almost eighteen.

They were there
staring aghast at that appalling release
into the wet bruise on the town's bosom.

THE RAILWAY CLUB

They were there again
showing their ID,
trying to charm drinks from the waitresses
still crying and being comforted,
having understood that there was something special
about this quiet lad.

"I should be proud really"
says his Mam, while toying with a *vol au vent.*

They were there with their flowers
like their pictures dripping in plastic bags
to see one of the Caia Kids
coming back home.
"See U Wen we get there"

WEDDING

The next day, a wedding in the parish.
A white limo and happy bells.
There'll be no chance for you to get
a lift in a ribboned car
in the order administered,
no chance for you to get this.

Today the happy chimes
ring out happy times,

and spring attires the one-day guests.

We can't escape from the morning bells
above the Town.

BINGO

(the following Summer)

"House!" yelled Mam
in the weekly lottery of numbers
down by Eagles Meadow.

She went back to join the girls,
although it was no longer her son
who came to check the numbers.

Everyone thought the world of him in Mecca
and Mam feels closer to him there.
Closer to that affection which transcended time.

Not a real *'full house'* anymore,
but a return to some sort of life.
Despite the laughter and shouting tonight,
the postponed inquest takes place tomorrow.

BEN 4 EVA

A young sister returns home,
she's back before the ten-thirty curfew.
Back to hear "Climb Every Mountain"
on the show to choose a new Maria.

The same looks as her brother.
She lights the fag of her youth
"D'ya wanna see the tattoo?"

Good work in twenty minutes,
colourful on young, wise skin.
Just one word,
BEN.

The graffiti's still out there in the rain today
The graffiti's still there on her heart,
her longing tonight is like a fresh tattoo dripping blood.

EIGHTEEN YEARS OLD

He didn't get to lounge around
by the bandstand, on the lawn of youth,
not even for a short spell.

On those fine days
when the gang goes loose-garbed
from the Caia to Llwyn Isaf
and when the sun is eternal
Ben wasn't there.

His Mam would stare at the other children
going past, carefree,
she danced a while with what-ifs
behind the nets.
Ben was deep under the heavy sod.

On an evening when the end-of-season sun sinks slowly
above Cyrn y Brain.

Tonight, Ben would have been eighteen.

THE BACK GARAGE

The Council came to wash the walls
and one of his friends protested
that the realm of live graffiti
was a token of respect.

The council worker had his erasing to do.

But he failed to see
the graffiti on the garage doors at the back
behind the shop.

That would stay,
when another autumn came,
with a breath of enquiry
to raise the leaves again.

The graffiti mountain
on the door of the back garage
went unerased.

BRON Y DRE

After Bingo,
while the weather permits,
they go up to tidy eight family graves,
and to crown them all
Ben's.

A sunflower standing tall in the border.

The season's first leaf strikes the screen,
and slithers slowly down,
acorns fall like manna from a bird's beak.

But on the New Lawn,
the golden inscription on the stone
"You don't know what you've got until it's gone."
Dan, has left another poem, in a plastic bag.
To think that Ben had been scared of him to begin with.

The picture of the teenager forever stares at us
from the silent stone.
The end of another school day
the roar of traffic rumbling below.
At the edge of the path,
Ben.

It's difficult to leave him there
with the insistent dance of his sunflowers.
A grave for his eighteenth,
the most expensive gift around.

Between the lines about what happened,
Mam is starting to come to terms,
starting to regain her strength,
and to realise that Ben's life meant something.

At the utmost edge of the town's cemetery
a hole so deep in hearts,
a hole from which there is no return.

The focus of your stone,
the image of your bike
on its eternal upward journey
from the Caia to the summits.

SPRING
*Leonard Cheshire established a Cheshire Home
at Dol-y-wern, in the Ceiriog Valley*

Conversion
above the harsh hell of Nagasaki;
Baptism in the shadow of the black mushroom.
You, Cheshire,
who'd been such a maestro
at the strategic explosion
that hit the target each time.

You, of all people,
exchanging the Victoria Cross
for the Cross of your Redeemer.

You saw,
beyond the extremities of man's callousness,
a vision that made you seek beauty,
and to strive for rebuilding,
to plant the seeds of love
worldwide
where once your destruction reigned.

From drunkenness came gentleness
the prodigal son showed his strength
and your nightmarish air raids
became triumphant crusades
for the world's needy.

Cheshire Homes
extending a loving hand over continents.
You raised, from the bitter bite of experience,
the crosses of your repentance,
memorials to your love.

Dol-y-Wern welcomed a Home,
symbol of your re-birth
and your Peace,
without roar of airplane more.

Only bird song,
river Ceiriog's accompaniment,
and the spring of your dedication,
blossoming hope
in long, trapped winters.

WALDO WILLIAMS
Welsh poet and pacifist from Pembrokeshire

He touched the Eternal once
between Parc y Blawd and the Weun,
remembered it in the dead of night
while the present howled at Tre Cŵn.

He saw the web between brother and brother
and countries that link hearts,
sought refuge once more in this palace.

A second only is captured in my photo.
The lens blinks astoundingly
and we struggle to understand
that afterglow he saw
from the sea of light.

ANDREA BOCELLI
Singing on the Square in Milano, Easter Sunday 2020

Grace shattered
the bleakness of the Square,
a ray of sun enters greyness;
Andrea's voice rising
as a phoenix from this pitiful situation.

Despite his blindness
here is one who sees
the resplendent towers of the Holy City beyond.

In the passion of his song
he embraces the unconquerable;
and the peace of the Ave Maria
showers through tears
on a virus,
and on all world strife.

VENICE AFTERNOON

"You must go to the backstreet canals
to see beyond the mask."

Sitting in midday shade on the steps of Salute,
the symmetry of passing Grand Canal gondolas,
and comforting lapping of water.
A retired tenor hits an afternoon note
that trembles the lagoon.

Back home they do not understand
why I come so far to re-connect.

I sit in the sun by Salute,
and shall venture beyond the mask
maybe
tomorrow.

RAMBLAS
Barcelona in Springtime

Leaves begin to bloom once more at Ramblas,
life's ceasless flow
beneath the tender blossoming.

Each one of us weaving our dreams
as the leaves begin to show.
Jump in the deep end, or drown by the shore
on Ramblas.

Young people embrace so warmly
as if the sun endears their affections
rather than complicates them,
when the leaves start to appear once more on Ramblas.

On days like these
I hope to continue to write and create,
like the opening of buds on boughs
on Ramblas.

CHURCH OF ST HYWYN, ABERDARON

Meeting God,
as if there is a roomful
brimming with pilgrims,
fervent of faith
ready to venture on the voyage
over the tempestuous Swnt
to that pearl on the horizon,
Enlli.
Bardsey.

Here we let the silence talk,
to feed us, weary pilgrims.
Here on the furthest tip of the peninsula,
where the centuries have offered
their souls to You.

Our aching feet
are washed in this atmosphere,
the beat-break of the wave calms
like our pounding hearts.

The invitation remains
to cleanse life's bitterness
in the spring of Ffynnon Fair,
and to go with faith on a voyage
to the island
that is always on the horizon.

CYMRAEG
Welsh

Seek to know more
of the secret
as old as the soil of Prydain,
Britain.

It does have to be natural to live,
like breathing,
shouted over streets
and in the rowdiness of pubs,
as language is.

It's not being rude,
it's just being.

It has to be natural at checkouts,
it was never designed to silence rooms,
but lies in a smile and fun
and a twinkle in the eye,
our shared Celtic beginnings
before Romans, Vikings, Saxons and Normans.

Welsh Government now wants
to double the number of speakers to a million.
Another half a million live worldwide,
but a new half a million within the borders of
Cymru
Wales.

It's not just there for show.
Gone are the conversations
"Stick the poster up there
and give people the impression it's alive,
but nobody really speaks it!"

Now they increasingly do,
and are entitled to services in
Cymraeg
Welsh
More than one language is now deemed
good for the brain!

Natural in the indigenous soil
of these Isles
in Dwfr, Ynys Wyth,
Dover, Isle of Wight
Catraeth, Glasgoed,
Catterick, Glasgow
Coed Celanedd, Ystrad Clud.
Caledonian Forest, Strathclyde
and featured somewhere near you throughout
Ynys Prydain
The Isle of Britain.

Tell your friends the real history
so that they are entranced.

No one should flinch
when they hear it,
be upset if they don't understand it.
No room should be so quiet,
no faces need redden
with our shared indigenous language.

No need to make eyes at each other
when you hear things announced bilingually,
that's called survival!

"We speak Welsh in Wales, so, get over it!"
the T shirt proclaims.
It's not spoken to keep others out
it's simply there.
It's not being elitist,
it's not a political football,
it should not divide schools,
but unify them when shared and learnt,
its cadences need to crescendo
down the corridors of all schools
in
Cymru
Wales

Jewel of these Isles,
Perl Ynys Prydain,
still spoken between young lovers
who will fight for its future,
raise their children to carry the torch.

CYMRU

Still refusing Edward's ring of castles
refusing the lavish penthouses in Abersoch and Morfa Nefyn,
where local people cannot buy houses in their own communities.
Aiming to give the indigenous language of Ynys Prydain
a voice in every school.

Instead of
the constant questioning why it exists.
What is the need when everyone understands English?
Turn over a new leaf
and simply now, let's live it
as we were always meant to.

EURWEN

Eurwen kept all the photos
because memories were treasured by her.
She captured our days in the album,
and was thankful for it all.
She so liked Geraint's energy filling the house,
when he and Carol visited,
missed him when he went home.

When we were on holiday in the South of England,
we went to Southampton docks
to wave you all goodbye on your QE2 cruise.
My mother and Eurwen had fun at Llanrhaeadr Show,
and ate all their winning cakes on the way home.

Eurwen was at ease in Llanfair Caereinion Stiwt
discussing her talented harpist aunt Nansi, and Cecil,
with pride and warmth.
That day Eurwen seemed a young girl again,
the days we treasure.

As a child I discovered a path from the back of Haytor Road
to the magnet of Eurwen's garden in Acton Gate.
We were all drawn to Eurwen
and she was a second mother to so many of us.

She had patience to watch my "Show"
and listen to my dreams.
She forgave the crash on the Chopper bike
when some of Uncle Gwilym's 78's were wrecked,
when I waved at her through the window
and lost my balance on the bike.

Eurwen was wise and understood it all,

as talented on the organ in Penybontfawr chapel
as she was accompanying the jazz band in Oswestry.

When David Kossoff the actor came to stay
I was allowed to interview him
about his films.
Then, I knew everything there was to know about films
with my Radio Times and TV Times cuttings.
I knew more about David Kossoff and his co-stars
than David Kossoff himself.

Photographs of the years have been kept,
you threw nothing away, but treasured them.
The good days are frozen in the shots
of that young smile
that embodied the mildness of the people of Maldwyn.
Always astute and striking,
always ready for the unexpected.

Eurwen recalled the minutiae of memories
with particular detail;
Similarly, she was insightful concerning people's feelings,
she understood which lines to keep and which could be crossed,
she appreciated the days.
Eurwen remembered all the connections,
and accepted the events of the years.

"Helo Al, sut wyt ti bêch?"

She was happy to see the good in each one of us.
and 'held the lamp' for us all,
with the sunshine of her smile and laughter.

GOOD SAMARITAN
Painting by Adrian Wiszniewski, Liverpool Anglican Cathedral

Naked wounded rebel on the side of the street,
and the unexpected woman from Samaria
offers balm at the inn.

Businessmen walk past,
clutching their briefcases tightly
in the darkest sky.

It's three o'clock on the watch,
and the menace of that hour
slithers slowly into the frame,
despite the refuge of the inn, and the wine's sweetness.

PALM SUNDAY

Country backlanes from Betws yn Rhos
to Old Colwyn,
are today verdant
like the covering of palm branches
and flowers
strewn at His feet.

O! that things could remain
like this victorious day;
that we could bottle
the crowd's earnest enthusiasm;
their unwavering loyalty,
like the colour of spring flowers
bowing on the roadside.

Shame we cannot drown
the sound of nails on wood,
with today's euphoria.

WITH THESE HANDS
Queen's Square, Wrexham at Easter

Hands reach for the bread,
hands tinged by the Cross.

At the end of the open-air service
we each put paint on our hands
then place our soiled hands
on the paper Cross
to remember our part in this heinousness.

Some chose the obvious red,
I, cowardly, am led to the blue,
to the hope that lies there inherent.
I chose blue to lighten the Cross.

Slowly the crowd disperses,
like dismantling a Cross,
sharing the guilt.

The Cross left on the Square,
with our hand stains upon it.
We escape with shattered consciences,
scatter from the town centre.

Without noticing that the paint stains
have already started to lift.

ONLY THE NAILING
Good Friday, looking at Craigie Aitchison's depiction of Calvary at Liverpool Anglican Cathedral

Quiet minutes with the painting,
and with the cold moon.

Then, nailing sounds fill the air,
the same old banging echoing,
nailing that hasn't changed despite all that technology,
that old basic banging of nail into wood.

All our priorities revolutionised
by the lashing of Love.

Recalling the day the Lamb was nailed by us,
not with words, or false excuses,
not digitally,
but with gruff voices joining the chorus;
that old nailing
in our complex make-up.

We raise our heads to Christ's victory in the centre.

Dark green below like the old tradition,
verdant green like the new covenant.
A sky of blood,
and both convicts each side, white.

RESURRECTION

For ages, I had thought that you were my resurrection,
the one who returned
after an absence of years.

For a long time, I thought that you were
the answer to life's puzzle.

But Jesus went ahead of the disciples
back to Galilee,
when he shook off his earthly shroud.

And now I know, that resurrection
is outside the familiar frame,
out there,
ahead of me,
always.

LLANDAF CHRIST
Epstein's 'Christ in Majesty'

Confidence is what I see in You this time,
the sheer fulfilment of the conquest of humility.
After all violence, each barbarity,
we must return
to this meekness.

You are adventurous in your gaze,
eyes set on the target,
in the glare of your new spotlight.

The Cross now dismantled,
You fly
in the victory of Resurrection.

We gaze up at you,
and you direct our vision
to aim for the goals of the Kingdom.

PENNANT MELANGELL AT EASTER

Primroses border the road
where the snow melts;
as if Melangell
has waved a gentle wand
along the old lane to the head of the *cwm,*
to help us access the deep abyss of Peace.

Think on that other road
which began in flowers
but ended on a cross.
A road which, alas, was not all flowers;
although the people
      with unsteady smiles
had strewn their boughs
just a week before.

But three days after such a dead end,
primroses bloomed
to shatter the grave.

SUPERHERO

"What do you wish?"
"Dad, I want you to be a superhero"
"I don't know if I can be a superhero"

"No, I've decided
that I don't want you to be a superhero.
I like you the way you are."

And they sealed a pact for life.

WELSH LEARNERS

Welsh learners use language differently,
in a fresh way
"Mae'n hyfryd dy weld di" *"It's great to see you"*
from the heart!

Welsh learners use archaic words
in enlightened ways
that makes them shine brightly again.
They enliven old idioms
"Dim rhoi'r ffidil yn y to." *They won't give up!*

Welsh learners enjoy discovering
for the very first time
the intricate connection between words.

From the storehouse of their diligence
they prepare for us delicacies.

We as tutors return home,
warmed through and through by their generosity,
and their love for our language.

PENNARD IN JUNE
In 1931 Dylan Thomas proclaimed from the walls of Pennard Castle. "They have rejected me now, but in years to come the name of Dylan Thomas will echo from shore to shore only I won't be alive to hear it."

Somehow Pennard
in the mist
doesn't quite work.
That stubborn old cloak
of drab days
precluding vision
beyond the heath.

I'm more familiar
with the Pennard of summer.
The azure sea
The three dazzling cliffs
and young Dylan's poetic genius.
The genius which challenged his father
not to slip gently into that final night,
and which saw,
for that one magnificent time,
that everlasting green
at Fern Hill.
A genius which insisted that Death
should not have the last word.

Clear, shining talent
not today's cloying mist in Pennard.
The fragile genius who once on a distant headland
asked whose company you would like
on the beaches of his day.

The muse which blew his energy onto the one-chance canvas of Llaregyb.

The brilliance in the unwavering Bay.

"THE PEACEMAKERS" KARL JENKINS
Llangollen International Eisteddfod

We return home along back lanes,
tears and stars mixing in our gaze,
confronted by all the possibilities of peace,
making our dancing feet
tap so lightly on Llangollen's pavement.
In the force of this music
we can confront an enemy and totally forgive them.

Here, there is no sense of failure,
and drowning in today's cynicism,
as we recall the sacrifice of
the Peacemakers.

Mother Teresa, Dalai Lama, Martin Luther King,
Ghandi, Nelson Mandela.
Tonight, they were the stars shining,
and although they have exited the stage,
they are somehow still with us,
in the corners of our perceptions,
in our haste.

Like possibility,
the makers of peace.

THESE
At the Llangollen International Eisteddfod

Those we defiled,
those we injured
those we wronged.
We were jealous of them,
Watchful of their tread.

Bruises which don't fade.

Those who fell
on the roadside of our experience,
who had no chance to explain
why things were like this.
Those we broke,
those for whom we were not a port
in the storm.
We did not shelter them from their night.

These.

They return
between folk dance and folk song,
to beg for justice.

They whisper the alternative long ago,
'Welcome to our friends from Germany'
'Croeso i'n cyfeillion o'r Almaen.'

WELSH POETS ON THE STREET

Student revision notes scattered
on the street corner by McDonald's.
Personification, and *metaphor* in Summer breeze dance.
Meirion MacIntyre Huws is recalled.
Revision cards
Style and appreciation
on the Ruabon brick floor.

I'm overjoyed that Welsh
has been scattered on this border pavement,
Welsh poets getting street cred!
Their verses no longer learnt for exams only
but released for all to marvel, on town paths.

Cymraeg for all to embrace.

Colourful revision notes:
Iwan Llwyd here set free in verse,
Menna Elfyn and Gwyn Thomas
labelled as *'totally vers libre'.*
How cool is that!

Simile, alliteration
personification, adjectives,
verbs, repetition,
personification, symbolism.

The relief of finishing
no need to memorise any longer for exams.
Homemade flashcards now scattered
to the four winds.
Thankfully the poem about the factory shutting
did feature on the paper as predicted.

Now pupils look forward to a Party
and farewell Prom.

Thanks to whoever,
scattered revision notes here,
because you have set Welsh poets free
amid the world of McFlurry.

Here, where the fast wheels of laden cars
this night will scatter their names.
On this one June night that is eternal.

SAME TIME EACH YEAR
An end of term meal with an A level class

We say that we'll meet up
every year on the same date,
because it's easier this night to say
that we shall meet,
rather than mention separation and distancing,
the change that will come in our idealism,
and to our sense of belonging to the Class.

But for tonight
at the end of the course,
we'll meet each year
on this date,
to continue this present union.
"Yes, Sir, every year on this date!"

We won't let the phantom into the party
take the edge off good company tonight
my lovely class.
Won't doubt for one second that
that's how it will be.

SURRENDER

I remember you in a school class,
the bad boy
who went out of his way to be awkward,
who could reply so coldly and clinically
to questions.
Detached and unfeeling
except for warm blue eyes
that told another story.

"Shit happens" was your motto,
but I could never totally disown you
despite your sermon on one exam paper
about how silly the question was,
and the subject,
discarding your ability to excel in answering the question.

I heard after
that the boy who walked
the borders of many a teacher's patience
had gone to see the world
in the name of defending borders and freedom in Iraq.

At a poetry reading years later
I happened to turn my head
to be greeted again
much politer this time.
Gruffness had mellowed,
and those blue eyes had surrendered
to the poetry within them.

SCHOOL REUNION

Familiar forgotten faces say "Hello",
Old fear and blushing of yesteryear
now lost in the maturity of today's perceptions.

It was hard to sing the last hymn
that last yellow afternoon.
We all placed wine coloured ties on the rack,
that cord that bound us all as a family
and gave us a land called Cymru
whether we were willing to take its responsibility or not.

Watching everyone joining tonight's dance,
I am dragged to the centre to pursue old moves,
old expectations, I laugh in all the old places.
"Dancing Queen, feel the beat from the tambourine..."

PONTIO

Pontio Arts Centre, Bangor was opened on the month that I was BBC Radio Cymru's Poet of the Month. These lines now feature on the walls and stairs of Pontio.

Yesterday, local pennies
bridged port and quarry with Penrallt.
A yearning chiselled from a generation's dream
of education for their children.
Their sacrifice was our privilege
as a path was created to the College on the Mount.

Today, a rainbow arc above the City of Learning,
bridges city and mount once more.
The Arts thrive here
in the dance of creation's cauldron.
Age old *Awen* stirs anew,
as it has bridged heaven and earth
since creation began.

Tomorrow, "Pontio" will remain
against all odds,
as a place where we,
like our forefathers,
sing louder, and proclaim
with gusto
the performance of our survival,
on that pathway striving for the stars.

BREATHE
Port Sunlight

Respect in each border,
respect for workers' homes,
Lever's thrift
transforming marshland into vision
with his big heart.
Benevolence
like the flowers of respect
still maintained at his grave.

But the marsh still emerges sometimes,
patches in the children's dell
that remain;
like hidden kindness in our world today
transforming lives,
hinting at the eternal.

It was an ordered freedom in the Village,
but still a freedom
from squalid city slums.
Several architects working
on living quarters with bathrooms,
spaces to breathe.

After the factory toil
places also for a community united together
in playing bowls for relaxation.
Uncle and Aunty Lever
gave the school and cottage hospital,
and perhaps most of all
the Art Gallery
with artefacts for all to behold
beauty,
to grasp eternity.

Birdsong and sprinkle of fountain,
the unifying peal of glorious bells.
Birth, marriage, death.
Unified.

Today's garden borders
are still respected,
and kept ordered,
although the sounds emerging from the homes
have changed, and the horizons within.

Now,
modern new factory and modern times
encroach on ordered lives;
green still offering
places to breathe.

AUNTY GWYNETH   Summer 1978

Each year with Wimbledon
came Aunty Gwyneth,
cigarette smoke and siesta,
eating out, and buying us hake for tea.

We laughed each time at her commentary
"That Tracy Austin
is so lovely I could eat her",
and the tales of her journey over 'Herwen'
in a Valleys posh accent,
rather than the Welsh Hirwaun she knew,
her Dad being a Humphreys from Corwen.

She only dusted off her Aberdare Welsh
for the old customers in Cwm Cynon Chemist
and the occasional service at Hen Dŷ Cwrdd,
she liked the Minister who came to have a sherry with her
now and then.

Len refused to speak English to her in Foel Isa.
"You Gogs wouldn't understand me anyway!
Luned my sister knows more Welsh than me
because her teacher in Aberdare Grammar was THE Kate Roberts."

Agreeing amicably with everything for her fortnight's stay
she responded "Quite",
like a Sunday afternoon tea in brittle china.

"New Balls please"
She watched the screen in her silk dressing gown,
her effects well-versed.
With us, she would smile each July.

Before,
that long, long road back over the long heath
over the Hirwaun home.
Each farewell a little more earnest,
her embrace frailer.

"You love us Gogs really!"
"Quite"

ERDDIG

The National Trust property in Wrexham where my mother worked as a guide in the 1970's and 1980's. The Yorke family had a tradition of treating staff as family.

The path back is longer than I remember,
through acres of estate,
until I see that familiar dovecote,
and the walled orchards.

I hear your voice immediately
greeting me from the kitchen,
welcoming me in Welsh.
You were the public's first port of call
in the "Waste not, want not" kitchen.

I would give anything
to sit with you on a quiet bench,
linking arms and chatting once more,
as we do in that evergreen photo.
Me, thin in denim.

My mother welcomed everyone with her smile.

Along the servants' corridor
she would wink at the portraits going by
each one with its poem,
and open side-doors between hidden passages
like a conjurer.

The Yorke family chapel is dark tonight,
a laden sky spreads its pale shadow
over familiar memories.

When I used to meet her from work
she'd open the gate of her heart for me,
let me in through the side door
of her trust.

Despite this being decades ago,
her smile still rakes the paths
and flies over stiles, with each new Season.

On quieter days
I return to Erddig to meet you again,
and to greet myself
in the cafe of yesteryear.

As shutters are raised to the sun
I discover again the trust in your eyes,
your warmth and your fun.

The servants' bells scream once more in the corridors,
yearning for your smile
that never fades.

GRASS CUTTING IN BANGOR IS Y COED

Each time I come
he's cutting grass by the church,
tidying the graveyard.
He whistles a tune,
and looks at me as if I was resurrected
approaching on the narrow path towards the Church doorway.

"It takes two days to do it properly,
and really I need an assistant."

We,
like cut grass,
present a silent prayer here.
He still whistles a vague tune when I exit,
his eyes probing
as if asking
what do I get from sitting in a quiet church.

Like grass ourselves
we will be cut and gathered eventually
for the next stage of the journey,
to the heart of Paradise itself.

BUTTERFLY
for Bet, Llanbedrog

To lie down for a while in the afternoons,
was the friendly guidance;
in that airy and light bedroom
where Bet's longing for jumping old fences
returned.
Her conversation was as lively as ever that afternoon,
like Bet weaving a tale on her way home from school,
on the rural lanes of Eifionydd.
Her fellow-travellers
regretting they couldn't hear the ending!

Relatives congregate
in the senate of the sitting room,
while upstairs a lovely breeze
tickles the white net curtains.

A transparent white butterfly flies in unexpectedly
through the gap between the curtain and the breeze,
it proceeds to savour the room.
"*Gad iddo hedfan!* Let it fly!"

It danced past learning, the collected wisdom of this locality,
past hidden talents on a road less travelled,
It settled with the naturalness of Bet.
"There's no need to hurry it on its way!"
Then her hearty laughter on an exceptionally sunny afternoon.

Inadvertently, the butterfly fled
through that strange abyss
between the shroud of the curtain
and the spontaneity of the breeze.
It flew confidently beyond this world,

having shed any dust from its wings.

"*Dyna fo. Dim ond dod yma am rom bach*
Mae o'n rhydd rŵan.
There we are. Only here for a short while.
It's been set free now."

PILGRIMAGE

1 Crossing to Hilbre

Beyond the sand's blinding stab
we must travel beyond the dunes.
Waiting for creation's old tide to ebb,
the natural rhythms of the day.

In its own time,
the tide allows
the slow, orderly procession
to travel to the jewel on the horizon,
as in the pilgrims' days.

Progressing slowly and gracefully
over the sands of time
to the gift that remains there in its silence
still not totally defined.

Always there on our horizon.

2 Basingwerk Abbey, Holywell/Abaty Dinas Basing, Treffynnon

In your peace,
in your silence
from the trudge of life.

In your simplicity,
in your magnitude
amongst hurdles and complexities.

In your permanence
in your survival

today when fickleness is rife.

You are a magnet
to revive and strengthen,
releasing us
to meet with God.

3 St Trillo's Chapel Rhos on Sea/Capel Trillo Sant, Llandrillo yn Rhos

The smallest church in the world,
a womb open to the ocean.
We bow our heads so low
in the six chaired sanctuary.

A well
now of messages
like echoes in shells,
Prayers of the empty tomb
collect expectantly, boldly,
the little waves mellowing their edges,
whispering the best kept secret of the shells.

Resurrection...Resurrection.

POOLS

No, they won't charge you today,
because all the brine pools
will be filled with beautiful clear water
that won't be too cold to bathe in.

The beautiful memories
which remain
without a ripple
within us,
so that we can dip in them
when we need to.

The pools of our yesterdays sustain us
and never run dry,
and help us conquer
the desert.

Today they won't charge you
all day long,
because everyone has earned their points,
and harvested their memories
to sustain them in the sun,
to recall on challenging days

Our memories remain,
just out of the direct sun's rays,
with a breeze from the estuary,
relaxing under the umbrella
occasionally looking out to the horizon,
observing any change in the tide.

SALEM
Llanbedr, Gwynedd. The chapel in Vosper's painting

I escape the busy avenues of life
and seek the ageless solace at Salem,
that spiritual shrine beneath summer boughs
by river Artro singing.
I honour tranquillity at Cefncymerau,
roam the country path
back to myself.

The Visitors' Book
is crammed with names from afar,
people who have yielded
to this peace within.

Gaze at the window in Vosper's art,
imagine Sian Owen standing in her borrowed shawl
on her immortal stumble to the pulpit.
Wonder at the Family Bible bold
which was her destination;
before gazing at protruding headstones
through open summer doors,
where butterflies play hide-and-seek
like souls.

Just a short break from ruthless timetables
to come here to Salem,
to meet that part of ourselves
which usually hangs on walls
like unquenched *hiraeth*.

Enter the wooden door,
corner your way to the pews.

Until the next time
you need to return
to the place untarnished by time,
to the chapel still in the hands
of the familiar crew,
always glad to see you.

Their weaknesses still apparent,
their forgiveness a gentle one.

DOLWREIDDIOG

My Nain's family scratched their need
from the thin soil,
bathed on scorching summer days
by the waterfall.
I should feel something here
in this rocky valley.

Newcomers nestling there
have no idea of this,
their dog barking at the gate.
Dolwreiddiog is not listed in the guide books.

The lane runs through my consciousness
back to this rugged scene,
where they struggled daily to school and chapel
miles away;
created their boundaries
with superb stone walls.

Boulders of my being.

FLUENT
In Trefaldwyn

Summer café with open doors and courtyard.
Smell of fresh scones,
shelves dripping with lemon drizzle cake.
Interspersed with talk of
"not feeling quite right the last few days"
and another's pending hospital appointment -
in the corner, there's an unofficial Welsh lesson
over coffee, here on the border.

"Mae 'na chwilfrydedd / there's curiosity am y Gymraeg
yng nghaffi Trefaldwyn".
Maen nhw'n gofyn iddi sut mae ynganu
"Lemonêd",
a holi pam mai Coffi yw Coffee,
ond mae ganddi ateb i bopeth.

The unofficial teacher praises the purchase of the red book.
Ac er iddi unwaith fod yn rhugl,
mae'r athrawes 'answyddogol'
yn canmol y llyfr dysgu coch,
yn gweld bod modd dysgu y lliwiau yn effeithiol gydag o.
y pethau a wyddai pan oedd yn rhugl.

Mae'n troi at ei gŵr
"You should buy one of these big red books.
But all the different areas say things differently
so don't worry too much.
It's a good book, mind."

"How do you say banana in Welsh?"
"I've heard Ffrwchnedd, but I always say Banana."

"Why do some people put an 'i' in the middle of Croeso
it makes it sound like Croieso"
"There is no i in the spelling."

And without realising she's unravelling the words
and the memories from when she was fluent.

She clicks the documents within her
those old files that have been lying there
waiting to be used.
These by far exceed the new text book.

"You know, the winberries in Llawr y Glyn
are wonderful,
the farmer still lets me go to pick them.
I phone him up "Den nhw'n barod?"
My mother absolutely loved Llawr y Glyn,
you couldn't speak English until High School,
wild flowers on back roads."
Then she recalls the farms
and the taste of Welsh
can still be traced like winberries around her mouth,
and soil under her nails.

"Diolch am yr help."

"Croeso" she says,
like someone who has been welcomed home.

The unofficial teacher is left
unravelling the memories and phrases.
That fluency
that is always intact within
at Llawr y Glyn.

CONNECTIONS
Dyffryn Tanat

Strings of belonging
from hedge to farmstead
so steadfast
so brittle
as these actual ties
which adorn the lanes,
leading the cows from
highland to lowland to be milked.

It wouldn't do to prodigally stray
to foreign farmyards!
Strings are raised and pulled down
when needed,
along ancient hedges.

Everything comes in its own time here,
the ties which bind us together,
this co-dependency on country lanes.
The cattle own the road, after all!

But within the confines of the cottage,
a realisation is emerging;
the storm hasn't fully brewed yet,
a storm that will shatter all the strings in its wake.

FOUR MORE SLEEPS

Four more sleeps
until my dream comes true.
Four more sleeps closer to you.

Four more sleeps
and perhaps Dad
will be here to stay.

Not arriving in the Close
in his big swank car asking:
"Where have you been hiding?
I've been looking for you"
And I know for a fact
that he hasn't done anything of the kind.

Four more sleeps
and perhaps I'll get to see
the cutest dog ever
that he promised to bring.
My sister tells me
"I'm sure he wouldn't mind
if you went over to stroke the dog."

But she doesn't see
that he's bringing the dog
to distract attention away from him.
From his absence.

He knows I love dogs.
He doesn't remember that it was me
who came to get him from the pubs,
to lead him patiently home.

Three more sleeps
and perhaps I'll get to see Dad
for myself
and believe that he's going to stay
this time?

DAMAGED

They are programmed this way,
don't know how to love.
Not really love.
They leave
and you can expect nothing more
than their debris.

They are the ones we are challenged to love
knowing it is futile,
but they off-load
their broken damaged goods in our lives.

They live their imaginary worlds,
created to defend them
from their wasteland reality;
and leave us with the broken crockery of their lives.

They'll forget your name,
slip in and out of identities,
disappear from social media.

People unable to love,
who need to lie and create an impression
which is so superficial.
People who easily disappear always to their next life
waiting already, always in the wings.

Damaged goods
fell off the back of the lorry,
as the lorry raced ahead to its next dream.
They will only ever slip through our fingers,
playing with our hearts, never giving theirs away.

We are challenged to love
the ones incapable of love for us.
The ones who will soon set off.
We are challenged to bring the broken goods home,
to wash their wounds.

But sometimes, only sometimes,
love is letting go.

MOTHER TERESA
by Gwyn Thomas

Eyes like a mother's eyes looking at her children sleeping,
or looking at them through a window, without them even knowing,
those are her eyes.

She's also called Mother
although she has no children
as other mothers have children.
What she does have is people with nothing,
the filthy beggars of India's streets,
lepers with gaping wounds,
children whose minds are sick,
the driftwood of the world's despair, and humankind's destruction.

What she also has
is Caring,
the caring that makes people brothers and sisters to one another.

She is Mother Teresa
the Mother who, in her own words,
is striving to accomplish 'something beautiful for God'
And amidst such a desert of pain and suffering
she has the contentment that belongs
to the ones called the children of God.

Translation Aled Lewis Evans

A CHURCH IN MONACO

Chatting, and looking at the ceiling
between exchanges,
amid the tidy splendour of Monaco.

We open our hearts
with the heavens above us,
contemplate our mortality,
talk of people who need treating
carefully.
Still God's shadow remains
in His ever-present heaven.

"I'd love to be able to believe that"
she says, pointing upwards.

Christ there ascended
welcomed to his Catholic heaven
by a sea of angels.

PLAYING FOR ME
Île de le Cité, Paris

I can't remember the tune
a nameless piece on your clarinet
- for me,
with the melodies
depicting the shared anguish of us all,
and my craving.

In your hat, greatcoat and scarf
the tune sounds out,
the notes penetrate
the depth of my being,
stirring emotions,
arousing them
and enticing them to the surface
as if dancing on the waters of the Seine.

Your melancholy notes purge the mind
cleansing and alleviating worldly fears,
the notes tonight rise as an echo from
Île de la Cité
giving hope to the 'bateaux mouches' and to me,
that there is a voice for all our sorrows
an expression of our despair.

Thank you tonight, young man,
for lightening this mind
and letting us share life's anxieties.

I could stay here for hours
              listening
to your balmy message,
older than history itself.

Sometimes sprightly,
sometimes gloomy,
an emphasis here, a lighter touch for the highlights.
Something sad to recognise your sorrow,
something moderate to bring us to one level,
something bright before leaving
to open the door on tomorrow.

You played for me today,
your fingers teased out the notes,
you voiced my despair.

translated by Martin Davis

INIS FAITHLEANN

As the morning mist rises on Cillarnie's beauty
I take the boat to the heart of Lough Leane.

"I'll come and get you in about an hour"

The boat slides away,
and I know for a while
that the island is all mine
to the accompaniment
of the eternal lapping
of innocent waves.

Let go of consuming fears,
like the medieval monks here,
who saw the same silver sheen on water,
chronicled their histories and tales
here in the university of the lake.

Reflections remain between water and cloud.

Inis Faithleann, Isle of Avalon? Ynys Afallon?
An island of bliss in life's despair.

Until
that age-old need returns
to stretch hands over water,
embrace the complexities that lie waiting;
and connect once more
with the possibilities of the mainland.

SIGNS
On a tourist bus in County Kerry, Ireland

Amid the jovial Ring of Kerry commentary
it was announced:
*"That's the village in this area
where the Irish language is still spoken"*
This is the area designated by government
to sustain a language's life.

*"This is where students can come to spend the Summer,
where they are sponsored to speak only Irish.
They even have to order their Guinness in Irish here..."*

The bus laughter dies within me.
Only one village on this western peninsula,
where the *Seanachai* is still known,
in this official isolation.

I visualise worse bus trips
in Wales Theme Park.
Pointing to Llannefydd or Ysbyty Ifan,
Crymych or Lledrod,
Bala or Caernarfon,
Llangwm or Llanuwchllyn,
and the commentator saying:
"That's where they used to speak Welsh"

Seanachai = storyteller

A NECKLACE OF STARS
*On a ferry trip in summer to see the nightlights of
Brooklyn, New York, the famous Statue of Liberty became
illuminated by an unexpected firework display*

A necklace in the sky
on a voyage in the dark.
Another normal evening for residents
of the city 'so good they named it twice',
but for us a night to view a carpet of stars
above towers on little Manhattan.

Our foibles and faults
tonight
are all strung out on a necklace of stars.
Diamonds upon diamonds.

With one ear to the hyped-up commentary
of the Frank Sinatra wannabe at the helm,
and the other tuned to the gentle lilt of the Hudson
a sci-fi film set emerged for the city of light.

To this gleaming Legoland location
impromptu fireworks shot above the Statue of Liberty
bringing an eternal spark
to our mortal dust under the stars.

Humankind and its cynicism, silenced.

The boat became full of little children
agog and vocal under the stars.
The ferry stopped on its voyage
and the captain himself came to the side
to open this unexpected gift in the air.

The sky a star factory
above the torch which welcomed the world.

Next day, I saw aspirations turned to dust –
stars trodden underfoot
on the gloss of Fifth Avenue.
Here, money buys transient stars
which fade and die.

ST. MARTIN'S IN THE FIELD

Tranquil
amid the pounding city's heart,
where once there were fields.

Only two or three
meditating silently this afternoon
in St Martin's Church,
that was once
on the green glades of the Thames.

Receiving the balm here
during this brief hour,
I am once more in the fields,
visitors have fled and silenced.
I sense Your closeness in this public place,
the geniality of Your company.

Here in the centre with You.
Here You bring our distant needs
close at hand,
and grant us a meaningful glance
at Your heart and kindness.

If You can be present in the middle of this,
You can be close in all of life's trials.
In You our hearts rejoice again.

Only a handful are taking photos,
they feel rejuvenated
by this brief communion with You here.

Like sunsets of yesteryear
on the glade beside the Thames,
St Martin once more in the fields.

THE GARDEN BEHIND THE THEATRES
Phoenix Garden, Stacey Street, West End, London

From the street's harsh concrete
where men lie in the corner of doorways
eating borrowed sandwiches,
from the constant din of traffic
finding you there is totally unexpected.
A walled garden behind the theatres
where children play freely.

Eden re-created with jumping and skipping,
sandcastles that aren't demolished.
Playing in shadow and sunshine
back in an age of bows and arrows.

A garden designed
to bring a safe heart back to the West End.
The phoenix rises here,
and people wish to be led back
to simpler days of collecting flowers.
They search for cotton grass,
roses and chives
to introduce to the Garden.
Children playing farmyard in the centre of the West End,
they shall always remember Garden days.

The elderly are coaxed
from the shadows of padlocked flats
to seek their favourite seats under the trees,
not always successful,
like life in the city race they stepped back from.

Official T-shirts declare
that the Garden is in full bloom,

certainly, wilder than the famous parks
ravaged by summer sunbathers.

The hum of traffic and squeak of taxis
is a little removed here, thankfully.
People slowly melt into conversation
in this womb of trust,
for there are new pools here to discover
of mercy and warmth
in the alcoves and arbours.

The Garden behind the theatres,
where the older child ties the laces of the small boy,
and everyone seeks paths.

You
are my beautiful garden
behind all the theatres.

TIDE TURNING
New Brighton, Wirral

Delightful
like a half empty fairground in the sun.
Another couple of turns
around the track,
it'll make no difference tonight,
it doesn't really matter,
before returning to face decisions.

Half empty rides tonight
a consolation
in our world of targets,
and the sun bright
on their alluring colours.
The Mersey undecided
on the turn.

No desire to leave New Brighton tonight,
just a desire to stay here
where sea and beach and promenade
are like a fairground ride.
I wish to stretch the elastic of these minutes
in the sun.

A beachcomber
is trying to sort something
from the tide's harvest.

New Brighton,
period,
as the tide turns,
and I must face the horizon.

STEREOPHONICS AT WREXHAM
Wrexham Racecourse Concert

I look from the sidelines now
from the safety of the stand.

In the swaying arms
and rhythmic jumping of the gig below
I see my yesterday also
swaying in the breeze,
shining in the splendid sunset.
I was there once, for a brief second
chanting the songs like everyone else.
"Local boy in the photograph".

Two mates from Chester enjoy their pints by my side,
one will be thirty next time,
but he's still asked for his ID.
"Keep hold of that" I say
"your youth!"
He desired to look older, for job interviews,
but when he gets to fifty, he'll be glad he still looks young.
"I couldn't hack it down there anymore"
pointing to the dancing throng.
After all he had got married and had a kid
all in the space of a year,
"How mad is that?"
Two mates enjoy their pints tonight,
let the excitement of the songs reign.
"Maybe tomorrow I'll find my way home…"

I smiled,
the tear in my eye shining.

There's promise of sunshine tomorrow
in the bleeding sunset over Cyrn y Brain.

"Have a nice day"

INDIAN SUMMER

Sparkling Indian summer,
gilded edges of old summers brightening horizons.
Why then is my heart so sad?

Ocean of light blue rhapsody
like the first chimes of Spring,
why then can't I ever be sure of you?

May's dance on the breeze today,
matching the image I have of you,
why then are you so changeable?

I long
for that true summer's day once more,
when the breeze blew so carelessly through my hair.

LAST DAY OF THE HOLIDAY
Barmouth

The day lasts long
as it did in childhood.
Everyone in Summer clothes
they waited long enough to wear.
Bathers of this last day
in the light meringue of the waves.

Slow down, and relax
before tomorrow's race,
before we jump once more
on that frenzied merry-go-round.

Enjoy that final ice cream
as the sun slowly sets in the bay,
its beams highlighting
handmade walls of farmsteads,
like the set confines of tomorrow morning.

This sunset shall sustain us
through all we have to do
once more,
for a while.

ABERFAN 1986

Screams of children playing
echo from the village below
in memory,
touching the edges of the children's graves
like thunder rain
spitting in puddles.

The scar of the white avenues,
show a generation lost,
buried in the careless sludge,
frozen in the black
one day long ago
in people's consciousness.

Except for the faithful few
who climb
to walk the white avenue on Sunday afternoon.
These haven't forgotten losing a son or daughter
on the altar of mute profit.

Screams of today's valley children
hardly feed their *hiraeth*.
And yet they walk with dignity
and Christ with them.

DESPITE THE SUN
Aberfan 1996 – thirty years on

There is no sunshine
even in May
that can mend the scar.

You must turn
from the by-pass to remind yourselves.
In the succession of generations
there is a fracture
that history will have to explain,
although today there's a shine
on the colourful terraced houses,
and young people once more
sitting on open doorsteps.

We must still look further
for that beautiful blemishing white scar,
that hides in the green fullness
of May trees.

There is still that *hiraeth* that remains
as coal heaps are still moved
and buried somewhere;
waggons rage
and JCBs today still
try to tear yesterday away,
like snatching a toy from the hands of a child.
The black slag re-emerges
where green had started to overgrow.

I smile tenderly at all the young
as we should do,
but they do not want our soppy stares.

"I'r rhai a garwn
ac y galarwn
o'u colli"
For those we love
and that we grieve
their passing.

An ice cream van from the Rhondda
sings a lullaby
"We'll keep a welcome in the hillsides",
its echo piercing
the gardens of neat little borders,
and gentle whisperings.
Thank goodness someone is skateboarding,
and a man takes his dog for a walk.

Despite the sun
"We're closing the cemetery, now, okay?"
White scar of a generation
amid ordinary graves
that seem more natural.
Not as harshly plain to see
as our media images,
but more a path through the forest.

There are graves above them now,
perhaps the children's parents
or relatives
joining them.

It was his last job of the day,
the council officer
locking the cemetery of Aberfan.
He couldn't wait to change into his shorts

and grab the rest of the May sunshine.

"I only came to see the graves."
"But we'll be closing now, okay?"

But it won't ever be shut
for the ones who still grieve.

The machines below still move earth
to try and tame
the bitterness of coal.

On a bridge up the valley
is written "Jesus saves".
Some in Aberfan
are still uncertain,
despite the sun
still shining today on Porthgleision Terrace.

EDITING

Don't edit yourself!
Let them see the full version,
before the drafting,
and before the spell-check.

Let them have the old spontaneous 'you'
without punctuation,
and altered tone.

Stop editing yourself,
let them see the bruising, and the hurt.

MINORITY

The minority language you see
is my world and life.
The one which accompanies
my coming and going,
The one that rouses a smile,
and the one that deals
with the secrets of my soul.
The language of entries and exits
and all cornerstones in-between.

The minority language you hear
is not a hobby I do,
or a waste of public money,
not a nuisance to put on signs.
It is simply the melody of my soul,
and within it my whole world revolves
in words and idioms and dialects.
It is my mainstream.

To understand this
you have to turn down country lanes,
seek societies in corners of pubs,
understand ethnic cleansing,
Welsh Nots and "For Wales see England".
You need a special kind of eye
that appreciates cultures
in gammy cafes, and mountain rescue,
in nurses' banter, in the whisper of lovers.

My language has always overcome
and was there in the beginning,
Brythoneg before the Latin, Norman and Saxon tongues.
And you, have obviously read different history books

that make no mention of this.

But the day has come to speak out,
to speak Cymraeg naturally in every sphere.

Help us breathe new life into your native tongue.

EQUALITY

We have to complain on her part,
draw attention to her lack on posters,
suffer English-only correspondence.

And all of this to be treated equally.

We have to play a game
'Spot the Welsh speaker'
in the unlikely corners, often without their Cymraeg badge.

And all of this to be treated equally.

We have to roam shops
and see any Welsh much smaller
(if at all)
beneath the ever-present English
because two complained that it was there at all,
and they had difficulty finding their Flora.

And all of this to be treated equally.

We listen to inane comments about our living language
"not being as useful as European languages",
and "We can't try it out on holiday" –
without seeing that it is crying for attention
on our streets daily,
and yearns not to be kicked in the gutter.

And all of this to be treated equally.

We have to phone managers,
and send letters that are never answered.
We enrage, swear sometimes,

smile, laugh emptily;
raise the question like a recurring Greek tragedy chorus
when a new shop or hotel opens
or after a shop re-furbish
"Why omit Welsh on new signs?"

And all of this, to be treated equally one day,
in our own country.

SCOUSE

The Scouse that day filled in the gaps
on the day that the links would be cut,
the day we leave Nathan in Liverpool.

Scouse burning the roofs of mouths,
rather than dialogue that would
ease this farewell, as he starts University.

We choke on Scouse,
let it burn the tops of our mouths
without letting on, that the tears are real.

SECOND CHANCE

"I thought it was a good time,
Easter,
Resurrection,
a new beginning"

I was so glad he called on Good Friday,
trembling with Easter Sunday surprise
I somehow recognised his knock.

A day full of crosses
was the celebration of his return,
small verdant leaves on the trees.

COULD HAVE BEENS

Why is my life
so full of could have beens?

Why didn't I venture through the snow
to Whitchurch that day?
Because the roads were slippery and uncertain,
and the thaw hadn't properly begun.

The place where emotions could have been neutral,
for both of us,
away from our settings,
perhaps the beginning of something.

My life full of things undone,
emotions not fully realised,
things unventured,
could have beens.

STARLINGS
Aberystwyth

They venture to the Bay as winter beckons, but no further;
curtailing their joyrides,
wanting no more than this imitating security.
In the warmth of their murmuration
loyalty hums beneath the pier,
above the black rocks
as the hoar frost bites.
The starlings who never thought to fly away.

Only their primeval cackle,
as they vent their eternal dilemma
to venture or stay?

At that very moment when the sun sets,
comes their loyal sway to sleep below the pier.

The starlings who never thought to fly away.

LONG ROAD
In remembrance of renowned Welsh hymn-writer Ann Griffiths who sadly died aged twenty-nine

That long, straight road.
Pontrobert in the dark tonight,
after an evening of remembering Ann
in John Hughes' Chapel.

Realising we have a long, long road
to travel home
after this brief hour
in the heat of the Flame that sparked
in this corner
many moons ago.

The furnace of Ann's inspiration
shaped on God's anvil once,
whetted in a cauldron of earthly grief.

Embers of her inspiration
are a balm tonight.
We hum her hymns,
as we inevitably return
on that long, long road
back to the town fair.

THE PHOTO

In memory of Mary Jane Davies, headmistress of Ysgol Bodhyfryd, Wrexham. Originally from Foel in Powys, who retired back there.

She personified *Mwynder Maldwyn*
that famous mellowness of Montgomeryshire people.

I was only with her for two short terms
so that I could get to know the local children
before moving to High School,
and I refused to sing in her choir for the Eisteddfod
because Welsh lullabies made me cry.

She taught us to make reed candles
and about their context in her Montgomeryshire.
I wrote her a story
about the ivy that crept all over the world,
and possibly controlled it,
and she was the first ever to say that I loved words.

Towards the end of her life
her relative told me that she kept a photo of me
on her hearth,
the boy who arrived from the seaside
to Border Town aged ten.
She must have hidden it
that morning I saw her briefly
in her retirement flat back in her native Foel.
I had arrived early for the village Eisteddfod,
and someone asked "Would you like to see your old headmistress?"

On that last day at Ysgol Bodhyfryd
she was tearful as well as us,
by the school gates.

She let the ones going on to the Welsh Secondary School
leave class before the rest that last afternoon,
the only favouritism she ever showed.
She had stored our sensitivities, and embraced them.

I almost spent a lifetime
without knowing
that my photo had remained on her hearth,
and in her heart.

UNKNOWN IN ARDUDWY

At the latest supermarket
when you try to purchase the Welsh regional paper
"Llais Ardudwy"
it comes up on the screen
as "Unknown".

Creating a face like a slapped arse
on the new till girl from the Midlands
with her false black fingernails
tapping the screen in vain.

Unknown?

No Mari'r Golau, Morgan Llwyd,
no Meirion Williams or flowers at his door,
no Bardd Cwsg, nor Salem and its shawl,
no Edmwnd Prys his Psalms to sing,
no Llanfihangel y Traethau.

VISITING YR YSGWRN
At the home of Elis Evans, poet Hedd Wyn

A day that is black
like a Chair's shroud,
angry clouds like a nation's disappointment,
the alarm in the Eisteddfod crowd.
Misty drizzle envelopes Trawsfynydd.

You can't send grey rain that lingers
to be re-built in St Fagan's,
nor the unchanging green of Cwm Prysor
and the dotted neighbourhood lights at night
from the front door of Yr Ysgwrn.

The darkness of the kitchen,
paper hanging from the ceiling,
with only the warmth
of hearth and coal fire
for comfort,
like Elis' muse.

Memories are kept warm by the family
who welcome world travellers here,
removing the black shroud in the parlour awhile
to unveil the Chair of chairs
crafted by a refugee from Flanders.

WAITING
Mary, Jubilee Road, Wrexham

We were waiting for her
in life and in death.
She'd always be late joining us in Church,
talking to everyone,
saying Hello.

And on her funeral day
we were waiting for her coffin
to come down the aisle,
Waiting for her as always,
as if she was trying to tell us something.

We were waiting for her
in life and in death.

Mary across the road has died,
and it's like the death of the street
in a way.
All the values of a cup of tea,
a helping hand,
looking out for each other's light.

Mary who gave me her key,
so that I could call anytime to see her.

And at her funeral
we were waiting for her coffin
to come down.
Waiting for her as always,
as if she was still saying Hello
to everyone.

The automatic light still comes on outside her house,
but no longer the light of her character within,
and all that remains
is the memory of all she had been to the street.

WELFARE HOUSE

A more civilized society
formed the Hall,
shrouded in unclear history now.
Like the dishes for all occasions
stored behind frosted windows
in old solid cabinets.

Old relics of giving and benefitting
with groups of women
mostly
smiling on wall photographs.

A sausage cushion
is all that keeps the keen winter's bite at bay,
preserves at the door the world of this place.
A brick keeps the kitchen door open.

We, elsewhere with our screens
penetrating our eyes,
yearn for peace in our hearts
and for simpler chilled times.

When there was time to drink tea from elegant cups,
smile contentedly in a photograph,
and to drop the latch as you leave.

WILLARD WHITE CONCERT
In memory of Paul Robeson, William Aston Hall, Wrexham

The concert became a worship of a kind,
that was far beyond the inert hopes
of a Friday night out.

Our fragile prayers
led by the sheen in the singer's eyes
and the wonderful voice.

Then, crystallised
in his quiet wish that any change
should begin with each one of us.

Our tears mixed
with rain turning to snow
as we left.

We were offered a pathway
to the soul of Paul Robeson,
led to his hearth
where the downtrodden of the world are welcome,
and war of any kind is refuted.

Continue to strive for their dream.
Live this reality.
*"Nobody knows the trouble I've seen,
Nobody but Jesus."*

HIGH BRIDGES
for Sheila Derbyshire

I always think of Sheila
on high bridges on the motorway,
as she didn't like heights
and diverted miles to avoid them.

Fox-like low November sunlight,
blinding,
but keeping winter away.
The final journey to see her.

She spent a lifetime of being kind.

I journey to see her at the cottage hospital,
the late harvest summer sun striking my eyes,
tearing us from our busy schedules.
Why hadn't we made more time sooner?

She was the lady who was there for us,
a friend at midnight;
when emotions were raw,
and loneliness weighing on us,
here was the dear lady at the other end of the line.

Today she was holding on to life
like the goats on the Great Orme,
clawing the cliffs,
like a child in a computer game
about to slip off the verge of existence.

She is content
although ill,
and asks me to come back again at the end of the week.

****

It's sunny once more,
but I know that this
will be the final time.

Fox-like sun, good to have it,
bare branches and the bite of the colours today.
I'm glad to remember sun
coming to see Sheila.

From the last wave
through the window of the ward door,
she also knew
that this was the final time,
waving her small hand
with all her might,
waving with all the energy she could muster.
A wave telling me to go on, and to enjoy my life.

****

Today Sheila
we're at the final earthly curtain.

She had sanctioned the running order
to truly reflect her,
as she looked after the minutest detail
in the stage props of our plays,
or the correct costume for children to wear.

Do you remember asking for that huge photo of Margaret Thatcher
from Brymbo Conservative Club,
concealing it in brown paper to bring it back to Rhos?

All for the sake of our drama!

You spent a lifetime being kind,
and tonight,
I feel the need to chat,
call by or pick up the phone,
but there is no one at the end of the line
tonight.

Missing my sharer of secrets,
there's nobody left now to remember these thoughts
we shared,
you made them count.
You made everything fine, and just normal.

Today again, the scorching sun at Pentrebychan.
Light blinds us again,
and eyes fill
for one who embraced us
amidst the minutiae of life,
and made our nonentity count.

Today's sun we can't hide from,
all is revealed,
face to face
as you cross the highest of bridges
without fear.

THERE IS STILL THAT FEELING

There is still that feeling
that Sheila will appear
unannounced
in a concert at the Stiwt Theatre.
And then she'll recall the story of her walk from home,
along the rocky road
and that some misfortune
had prevented her coming
to the last concert.

There is still that feeling
that Sheila will pop into the Co-Op for a tin of salmon,
and come out hours later
having spoken to everyone there,
spoken from the heart.

Her endearing, fulfilling chat,
her promise to call around someday,
before the gentle farewell touch.

There's a local drama in a village hall tonight
waiting for a costume, or a special prop,
so that everything will look fine.
"Don't start Act Two without me,
I'll pop home to get it!"
We're still waiting for Act Two to begin.

There is still that feeling before Christmas
that Sheila will call by the warden-controlled flats,
or the hospital ward,
with an arrangement of flowers she has selected
together with the sunshine of her smile.

Only the roar of the wind tonight
wanders the close streets of Rhos.

But there is still that feeling that she may call by,
or that we can just pop in and see her,
or share our latest woe and happiness
on the midnight phone call.

Sheila is not there tonight
at the other end of the line,
on the hotline to her patience and understanding.
No answer tonight.

Now she is in her Father's House,
in one of its beautiful mansions.

That's the only place Sheila can be,
on a night like this.

NO MAN'S HEATH

Every journey east is a journey into the unknown,
to border villages, to the old pangs of history.
Mist lingers all day at No Man's Heath.

Was it here that every border was invented
each *entente*, each truce?
To establish Wales here, and England there,
that unwritten agreement written on the wind tonight?

Stalemate conversations suffice
in No Man's Heath Diner,
discussing every leaving and every arrival,
embracing every border that ever existed.

Here the border breathes independently,
comes to its own in the night mist,
digging its claws into your soul,
seeking loyalty on both sides.

I'm weary of this old, long road
running through the centre of No Man's Heath,
this border tightrope;
I want to find my way home,
to follow a light back over the border.

In which direction will you go, late traveller,
on these border lanes?
Can I follow your enticing light?

TELL ME ON A SUNDAY...PLEASE

He's traded me in for a younger model.
He just came home
and said 'I don't want any tea,
we have to talk'

He doesn't take his new woman
out anymore,
so someone said.

Why tell me on the day of my insulin test,
and just before tea?
Why didn't he tell me on a Sunday
after thirty years?
Tell me on the day
we always had a long walk along the canal
and over the aqueduct?

If he'd have told me then,
we could have talked things through,
not "We've got to talk"
before tea on a weekday.

He still comes to check his e-mails,
leaves money for half the bills,
comes to see his cats.
Why would I change the locks?

I might tell him next Sunday.

ADVENT IN CHESTER
Walking by St Werburgh Cathedral

This night's congregation within,
safe behind the reflections of stained glass colours.
A local private school with its select congregation
celebrate Christmas early
before the students scatter homeward.

Then came
"Hark the Herald Angels Sing"
and passers-by like me
on this night, frosty underfoot,
we listened.

The stabbing stilettos of the giggly girls
on their way to the Club subsided,
Sausage fryers on the Christmas Fair
raised their gaze from their chores.
Paused, not wishing the carol to end.

We listened to voices and trembling organ,
descant flowed through the walls,
as if the cathedral was fit to explode
on to this frosted street.

Caught in wonder, we were as children,
as if we could see angels,
and that the shining star on the Green
was a real Star.
For a while we were in a land
where we understood the shepherds' surprise,
and elderly kings embarking on an arduous journey
to the cradle of a Baby.

For this time, the heavy wooden doors that divide
were like the rustle of angels' wings,
and a melody flowed amid our fragile and quarrelsome humanity
stating that Love could overcome the world.

"Glory to the new born King"

CHRISTMAS CONCERT AT THE PARISH CHURCH

Loud and awkward shuffling
to clonky wooden pews in stilettos,
the tuning of instruments.

The accompanist looks far too important
to say the least.
The struggle to ignite the Christmas tree lights,
the ordeal of getting the spotlight spot on.

It's a new take on the old story,
programmes are distributed,
dresses are straightened
murals of angels blush above.

Then,
after seven
when the concert begins,
the angels above soar
like miracles suspended,
and innocent wishes
are about to be realised.

EAGLES MEADOW FOUNTAIN
Wrexham's shopping centre

The coins were tossed in the gushing fountain,
each with a wish beyond confines;
That day the foamy water sparkled,
and there was a rainbow in the turn of the coin.

But today, the fountain is dry, the coins are rusty,
the sediment of chemicals in redundant pools.
Eagles came today to feast on dreams
tossed in the fountain one sunny yesterday.

LIGHT
for Frazer when he was six years old

Frazer reads to me from his Bible,
wiser than his years,
He's so proud of his collection of stories,
and engrossed by all things Egyptian.

He still reads
when his brothers' lamps
have been switched off
in the bunk beds.

He knows all the characters by name,
reads with his torch on the pillow;
but he doesn't like the picture of Jesus
with the crown of thorns on his head.

Frazer clings
to the Light that won't extinguish
devouring its nurture
in the night-time darkness,
at only six years old.

MAIR COEDPOETH

"Alan, my son, asks me how I am
and I tell him 'My mouth's alright'."
Mair loved to chat.

"God's not asleep"
she often said
"Dydy'r Brenin Mawr ddim yn cysgu"

There is no chat in the bed we are beckoned to,
"Don't try to talk now.
You've talked enough."
Her son tenderly touching her arm,
an old understanding, and love.

He looks at her hands,
those hands that have given.
Hands that worked for ministers
at the organ,
and with food in Salem vestry.
She kept a welcoming hearth
cared for her family,
and contributed to Societies
and Sisterhood at Salem.
She helped during her life
where she was needed.

No chat today
only an upward gaze to another land,
a head-on gaze,
as on the paths of the years;
she faced the next life
with confidence
as if familiar faces

were coming to meet her.

Her deeds spoke volumes.
Giving.

Giving too much.
Dinner on a plate,
bread to go,
another piece of cake,
and always plenty of tea.
The welcome at 66 High Street was proverbial.

In God's Kingdom
we can't give enough,
and every giving is a gift to Him.
And in a world that only takes,
these people are the salt of the earth,
giving life its taste,
and when they leave us there is such a chasm left behind.

No chat today Mair
because you're on your way
to meet the *Brenin Mawr*
the God who never sleeps.

THE MINISTER
by Rhydwen Williams
Dedicated to Rev Harri Williams of the Rhondda Valley

He had the strangest notion about mankind –
you'd certainly believe he was dreaming
when you heard him praising,
only that his eyes were still open
like windows embracing the dawn.
He saw them pure like priceless gold,
the schemers, the fighters, the cranks,
and shining with virtue
as beautiful as the rainbow
that bridged Rhigos and Hirwaun awhile;
there clearly, without being there at all.

He gazed at the needy
young and old,
not as one too innocent to know better
but as one who beamed his own honesty
into life situations.
Nobody would think him successful in the fairs of today –
his modest dress and body language,
his good manners, his innocence and his smile,
his pastoral concern for the area,
and loyal to his Sundays
without worrying about payment.

He brought the Word
to congregations in old, cold vestries,
his face pale there
as his breath froze on his lips,
and only his prayer giving warmth.
But when he was around
it was a beautiful world –

as if the apple was still on the bough
and the serpent had been dispensed with forever
and only virtue our choice.

Despite this, we took him for granted;
the sound of his footsteps on the pavement,
his depth, his humour and his talent
and his voice on stage and on our hearths.
But in him was that virtue
that has been declined and forgotten by us,
the good that only poets and small children
recognise and acknowledge now.
His magnitude was to display for us
this innocence in a land
where life was shipwrecked at our feet,
shoulder to shoulder with the people.
The world is so cold, he used to say,
and what other way is there to keep warm?

Translation by Aled Lewis Evans

FINALÉ

"You've never learnt your lines"
said the old director
there for his last performance.
His words directed with love
for the actress whose career he had nurtured.

He was looking to that cruel last curtain,
but she still held an annual Panto in the chapel vestry.
Carmen in a vestry! Only she could pull that off!
He remembers how he saw such a talent in this girl
who had ad-libbed so skilfully in every show.

But tonight a tear emerged spontaneously,
that stage direction higher than all the scripts
that dwells in our age-old drama since the beginning.
It bounced down both their cheeks
as they took off the make-up.

And she knew the script perfectly.

REUNION

Ten years on
a pub crawl of apple juice,
sparkling mineral water and Diet Coke
around some of the adolescent landmarks.

From Fat Cat to the unchangeable Golden Lion
locked in the memory.
On our journey
from behind the Christmas decorations
we pluck memories of fun at school,
the madness of collecting coursework,
teachers and their idiosyncrasies.
Anecdotes
from that eternal land,
where we were all once with each other.

Seeing the past from a different angle,
Seeing the butterflies
that emerged from their chrysalis confidently,
but with shades of the shells of yesteryear
remaining.

We promise to do this again.
Next Christmas.
"Well I'm going to leave you three young ones
to get on with the rest of the evening now,
so that you can have a proper chat."

And after the remembering, and their respect,
the minute I turn my head,
the three escape for Liquid nightclub,
like three mischievous pupils on corridors long ago.

The lovely three, pupils again,
for one night only,
and I am once more "Sir".

THE ONE

The Christmas card not in the collection,
despite the attempt at a neat display,
the card that doesn't adorn the shelf.

That card not there
due to circumstances,
a difficult busy time,
or being unable to respond
in the rush of things.

The card that doesn't fill the festive frame.

Perhaps not intentional,
this void in life's desert at this time,
we may reach an oasis.

We imagine the display complete
and remember the person,
their part in our hearts.
Perhaps next Christmas we can complete
the collection,
when things are easier,
and the road clearer.

That one card that is not there
that hurts to the core.

WAITING IN THE WINGS

*"Where do broken hearts go,
can they find their way home?"*

He's going to be living all that,
when he realises
that there's more,
always waiting in the wings.

He knows about it,
but like several of us
hasn't really faced it.

*"And if somebody loves you,
won't they always love you?"*

Instead, he always hurts others
before they get a chance to hurt him.
The beast within him in conflict,
always waiting in the wings.

WHERE WAS JEREMY KYLE WHEN YOU NEEDED HIM?

On the screens,
dreams of Australia, and DNA tests,
Lie Detector, and beaches of escape,
but the reality for the runner on the Gym treadmill
is different.
Jeremy Kyle, or what's lurking in your attic?
Before he returns to the reality of the deception.

Fly on the wall television
created to highlight the morning.
Peter now happy, Jordan not so sure.
Piers saccharin-smiled now
with ones whose careers he shipwrecked once
in tabloid past.
Attic and argument, and beach with no roots.
Blood pumps along his arteries,
pumping more intensely because she has moved out.

Makeover programmes on the gym walls,
everything transformed apart from our problems.
On the treadmill he watches but he is losing weight each day,
he no longer puts the ring in his nipple.
No need to impress and fake-tan anymore,
now that she has gone.

He watches this moving wallpaper world
but he is living the real thing.
He can't relax his mind from the images she put there,
he needs counselling, so he says,
Barbie's name still stretches on his neck tattoo
as he runs.

In a tabloid TV world
where you can't look at a child without being a paedo,
nor be generous with someone without ulterior motive.
He wants to vomit on his empty stomach
and his aching abs.

"Sex with the ex" comes on
he watches mute lives,
and knives hiding in subtitles
as he raises the weights.

He runs a bit harder this morning
back on the moving track
to lose himself more,
to keep reality at bay.

Gym time is a small island in his life
without pain.
From "No Pain No Gain Gym" it's back to his world,
his Barbie tattoo redder than usual
after the shower.

He's sick of constant re-runs.
Where was Jeremy Kyle when you really needed him, anyway?

MARY AND JOSEPH IN SPAR

Mary and Joseph
are down in Spar '8 till late'
warming a cheeseburger
in the microwave of the moment.

Bus strikers are in their make-shift cave
by the picket fire of their resolve,
eavesdropping for a sign tonight.
seeking a flourish in the heavens.

You'd expect that dream factory
of a television studio over the road
to offer something this lonely night!
Import some exotic guests from far off lands
for their Christmas schedule.

But they are far too busy
massaging their egos
in the emptiness of mirrors.

There is nothing newsworthy any more
about Mary and Joseph's plight in Spar.

If only someone would look at the couple,
and that newly born baby
in the mother's arms.

KEEPING THE IDEA ALIVE

There's a bitterness in the sea today,
that bites beyond our worries
to the core.

But I have kept true to You
to this warm presence in my heart,
kept to it
through the mayhem of trying to strip You
of all Your wonder.

I've nurtured Your closeness,
and lived with You
through the winters.

Hoping again this year
that the warm parcel of Your grace
will flourish within me,
like early petals on blossom trees
innocently waiting to welcome Spring.

DARREN

In memory of Darren, one of the leaders of Caia Park Venture, Wrexham

A loss always cuts deeper in Winter.

At a time of darkness
with ribbons and January wreaths
on the side of roads,
trees without leaves,
prickly bare hedges.

On such a time you left us,
the gentlest of Caia Park's sons,
one who looked after others in the Venture,
their Daz.

He gave youngsters meaning in the barren nights,
made them proud of where they came from.

Far from Pentre Gwyn
by the Afon Wen you left us,
this fatal accident took the Gwenfro hero.

I remember you in my registration group in school,
when January wreaths are prickly on the sides of roads.

But there is always a field of sunflowers
dancing in a Summer breeze for you
in the hearts of Caia's children.

REQUIEM FOR EMMA

"There was no need for her to do that, was there Sir?"

A young death casts the darkest of shadows
down the cleanest of school corridors.
Emma, child on the fringes, always waiting in the wings,
a quiet dear angel aged only seventeen.

I have one photograph of her
through a radio studio window with her head bowed
shying from the Media Studies photo shoot.
Some are too gentle for this world.

Hearing of your death
is like April petals thudding silently
on a hard, relentless pavement;
or icy Minera wind disturbing Spring.
Your uncle remembers you in snow there,
the pure snow at the start of the stream.

I remember you as a little girl
amongst streetwise ones,
Remembering how you feigned being tough
to blend in, only sometimes.

You chose Barbara Windsor for your project.

Remembering your uncertainty,
not wishing to burden anyone;
Noticing the first time you put make-up on.

We all hope you are out of your dark cloud now.

The first song at your funeral
was like dance night
on a weekday at Bonkers Nightclub.
The second hymn by Macy Gray,
and then "Goodbye"
for the girl who had doted on the Spice Girls.
Baby Spice.

We cannot answer all the questions Emma,
only present a silent requiem
to your gentleness today,
knowing we lost it too soon.

A sunbeam shoots
to melt the stubborn snow
in Minera, Gwynfryn, Bwlchgwyn.

VALLE CRUCIS ABBEY

Hub of that quiet, tireless learning
whose truths shone
beyond the narrow valley of the Cross.
Through the arch of the past tonight
I'll approach the peace which sustained
the ancient bards and rhymesters
in good times and in bad.

An abbey which was a constant light in our darkness.

Before the valley became populated,
seconds to experience the peace
which is older than the voice of Oernant.

Listen to the evening birdsong
the sudden commotion in the fishpond,
and tonight, I'm probably the only guest
in the refectory of the good old days.

FLOW OF DIVINE DEE
In memory of Mary Gertrude Jones, Pantrhedynog and Frondeg, Glyndyfrdwy

There was no screech of train in the valley
the day she left.

The flow of the river was vigorous
bursting its banks.
January's naked branches
framing the tempestuous water
in her beloved garden.

On a day when the river was vibrant at Frondeg,
the flow of her life left Glyndyfrdwy,
a half moon reflected above.

In weak winter sun,
following a life brimming over till the end
at Frondeg and Pant
and at the chapel on the edge of the main road.
She left quickly and contented
from the triangle of her life,
the river a soundtrack to her days.

She had witnessed its seasons
in the same house on its bank since marrying,
for seventy years.
Her smile remains to fill the void,
at all the meetings.

No need to water the garden tonight Mary,
you watered all your days.

And when Spring and Summer growth

revisit the vale of the divine water,
verdant evergreen memories of her
will be ready to pick from the orchard.
Apples will be ready for apple tarts
and vegetables grown from seed to enjoy.

In the yellow sunshine of harvest
there will come a time for us who remain
to chat and reminisce,
when the river's flow is a meditation.

There was no screech from the train in the valley
the day she went.
She knew, farewelling,
that there would always be better days to come
for those who had watered the good days.

THE ANGEL
Ynys y Brawd, Barmouth

Beyond the sand's blinding stab
we must travel beyond the dunes to the Island;
beyond the brittle shells shattered on life's concrete
the Angel awaits,
like the sturdy coastline grass,
her finger pointing to horizon beyond horizon.
Her smile like the assurance of old sunsets
reflected in evening windows of the mainland,
like the soothing cry of the estuary bird
that reverberates in our winters,
echoes that have stirred since the beginning.

Crossing to the Island
possibilities are hidden in her wings,
their familiar shuffling pacifying our storm
as we escape the noisy seagulls' bickering,
scrapping for the biggest piece of bread.

The Angel is hermit-like in candyfloss summer,
her dialect unintelligible,
but once the fierce currents return
at the end of the winter line,
she sits like a beacon of light,
her rays winking at me.

Once again she is gazing at the horizon beyond horizon –
we can only begin to visualize
priceless treasures
that will illuminate our pale vision there.

Index to Titles of Poems

A Church in Monaco	81	Indian Summer	94
A Necklace of Stars	86	Inis Faithleann	84
Aberfan 1986	96	Keeping the Idea Alive	142
Aberfan Despite the Sun	97	Last Day of the Holiday	95
Advent in Chester	125	Light	129
Andrea Bocelli	29	Llandaf Christ	44
Aunty Gwyneth	60	Long Road Ann Griffiths	109
Ben from the Park	16	Mair Coedpoeth	130
Breathe	58	Mary and Joseph in the Spar	141
Butterfly for Bet	65	Minority	101
Christmas Concert Parish Church	127	Mother Teresa	80
		No Man's Heath	123
Church of St Hywyn	32	Only the Nailing	42
Connections	75	Palm Sunday	40
Could Have Beens	107	Pennant Melangell at Easter	45
Cymraeg Welsh	33	Pennard in June	48
Cymru	36	Pilgrimage	67
Damaged	78	Places in Wales	13
Darren	143	Playing for Me	82
Dolwreiddiog	72	Pontio	57
Eagles Meadow Fountain	128	Pools	69
Editing	100	Ramblas	31
Equality	103	Requiem for Emma	144
Erddig	62	Resurrection	43
Eurwen	37	Reunion	135
Finale	134	Salem	70
Flow of Divine Dee	147	Same Time Each Year	54
Fluent	73	School Reunion	56
Four More Sleeps	76	Scouse	105
Good Samaritan	39	Second Chance	106
Grass Cutting in Bangor is y coed	64	Signs	85
		Skateboarding	14
High Bridges	118	Spring	26

St Martin's in the Field	88	Unknown in Ardudwy	112
Starlings	108	Valle Crucis Abbey	146
Stereophonics in Wrexham	92	Venice Sunny Afternoon	30
Superhero	46	Virtual	15
Surrender	55	Visiting Yr Ysgwrn	113
Tell Me on a Sunday…please	124	Waiting	114
The Angel	149	Waiting in the Wings	138
The Garden Behind the Theatres	89	Waldo Williams	28
		Welfare House	116
The Minister	132	Welsh Learners	47
The One	137	Welsh Poets on the Street	52
The Peacemakers	50	Where Was Jeremy Kyle When You Needed Him?	139
The Photo	110		
There is Still That Feeling	121	Willard White Concert	117
These	51	With These Hands	41
Tide Turning	91		

FURTHER PUBLICATIONS BY ALED LEWIS EVANS

ENGLISH POETRY AND PROSE
Driftwood 2010 Short stories. (Gwasg y Bwthyn)
Someone Else in the Audience 2012 Poetry (Gwasg y Bwthyn)
Harvest Tide 2019 (Novel about Barmouth chilhood – contact the author for copy)

INCLUSION IN ENGLISH ANTHOLOGIES
Chester Poets anthologies (Cestrian Press)
A White Afternoon (Parthian) 1999
Bloodaxe Book of Twentieth Century Welsh Poetry in Translation 2002 (Bloodaxe)
The Old Red Tongue: Anthology of Welsh Literature (Francis Bootle Publishers)
The Creative Freedom of the Mind (Viva Voce Publications)

RECENT WELSH LANGUAGE PUBLICATIONS
Amheus o Angylion (Barddas) 2011 Welsh poetry
Llwybrau Llonyddwch (Gomer) 2015 Paths of Peace in Wales
Llinynnau (Barddas) 2016 Welsh Poetry
Tre Terfyn (Gwasg Carreg Gwalch) 2020 Welsh prose

Some of the recent books are available on gwales.com
For limited copies of earlier Welsh books from 1989 contact Aled Lewis Evans on Facebook, Twitter, or Linked In.